FOOD
for thought

FOOD
for thought

The complete book of concepts for growing minds

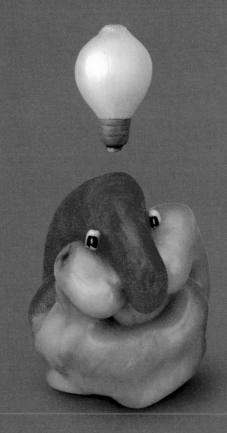

Written and illustrated by Saxton Freymann

SCHOLASTIC INC.

New York Toronto London Auckland Sydney
Mexico City New Delhi Hong Kong Buenos Aires

For Devo and Abi Ihonde

ISBN 0-439-78895-1

Copyright © 2005 by Play With Your Food, LLC. All rights reserved. Published by Scholastic Inc. SCHOLASTIC, the LANTERN LOGO, and associated logos are trademarks and/or registered trademarks of Scholastic Inc.

Arthur A. Levine Books hardcover edition published by Arthur A. Levine Books, an imprint of Scholastic Inc., February 2005

16 15 14 13 12   16 17 18 19/0

Printed in the U.S.A.   40

First Scholastic paperback printing, September 2005

Book design by Elizabeth B. Parisi and Saxton Freymann
Photography by Saxton Freymann and Nimkin/Parrinello

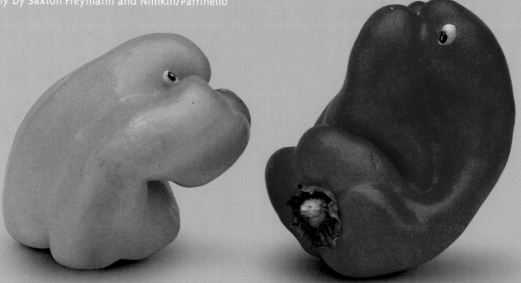

Ingredients: oranges, kumquats, rhubarb, black-eyed peas, assorted broccoli, bell peppers, onions, carrots, portabella, enoki and white-button mushrooms, sesame seeds, mustard seeds, pink and green peppercorns, red grapefruit, kiwifruits, cauliflower, spaghetti squash, starfruit, apples, leek, jumbo scallion, beet juice, strawberries, black beans, lemon, black rice, damson plum, concord grape, Chinese eggplant, sweet potato, black olives, pear stems, artichokes, yellow squash, assorted pears, bananas, cherries, baby pineapples, green Italian peppers, eggplants, brussels sprout, baby corn, bok choy, tomatoes and plum tomatoes, radishes, peaches, endive, assorted cucumbers, beets, celery, blueberries, onion skin, persimmon, pomegranate, mango, broccolini, papayas, snake squash, watermelon, acorn squash, asparagus, zucchini, canary melon, lady apple, nectarine, potatoes, parsley, turnips, fig, okra, daikon radish, jalapeño pepper, honeydew melon, savoy cabbage.

Table of Contents

SHAPES

Circle

Oval

Triangle

Square

Rectangle

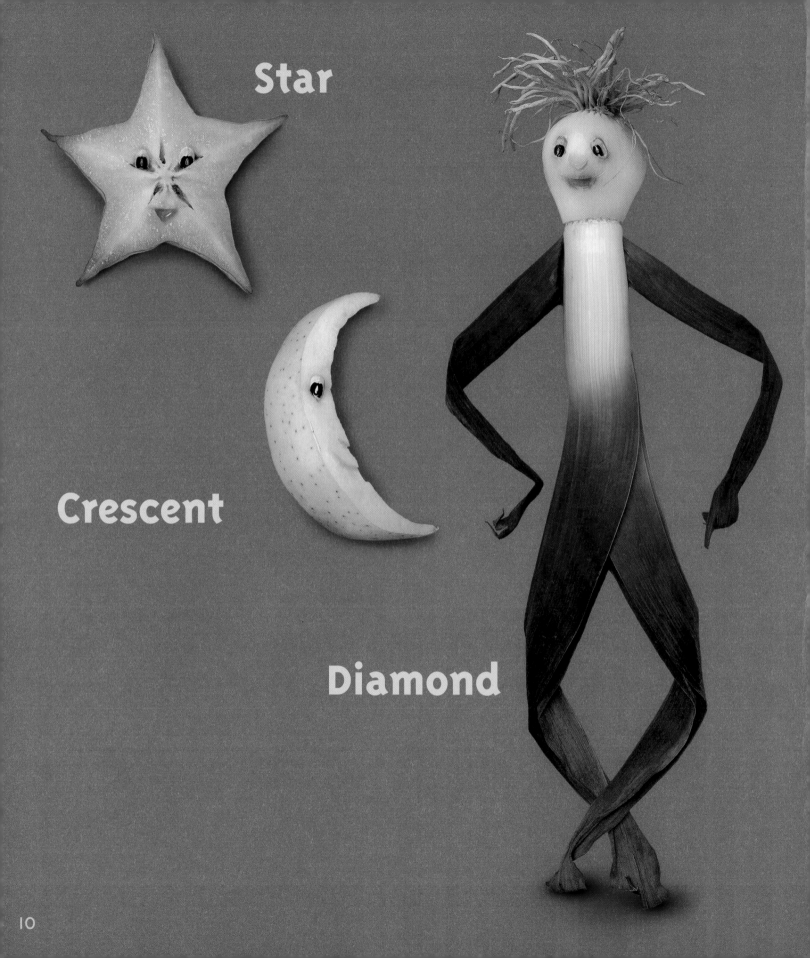

Star

Crescent

Diamond

10

Heart

COLORS

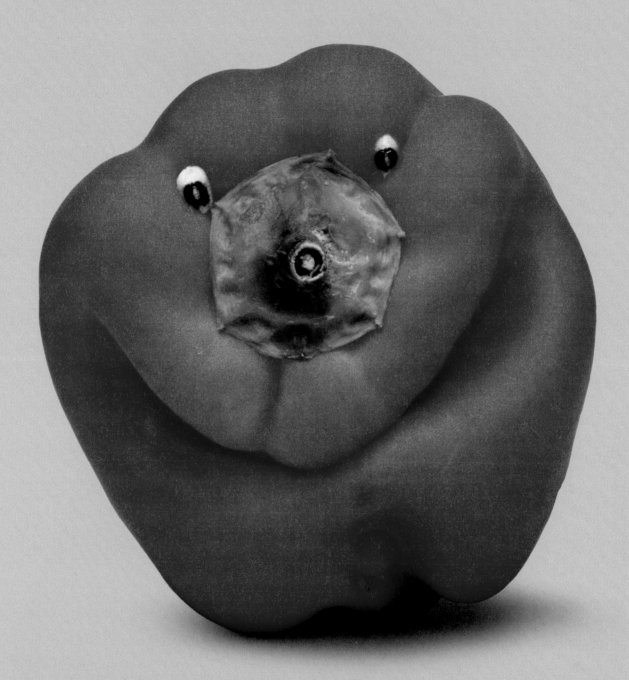

Red

Orange

Yellow

13

Green

Blue

14

Purple

Brown

White
&
Black

COLORS!

NUMBERS

1
One bird

2
Two chicks

3
Three giraffes

4
Four ants

5
Five turtles

6
Six penguins

7
Seven fish

8
Eight hippos

Nine frogs

10
Ten sheep

A a
Airplane

B b
Bird

C c
Cat

Dd

Duck

Ee
Elephant

Ff
Flower

Gg
Guinea pig

I i
Insects

Hh

Hair

39

Jj

Jack-in-the-box

Kk
Kangaroo

Ll
Lizard

Mm
Monkey

Nn
Nest

Oo
Owl

Pp
Pig

Q q
Queen

R r

Rabbit

S s
Snake

T t
Turtle

U u
Umbrella

V v
Vegetables

W w
Walrus

X x
X-ray

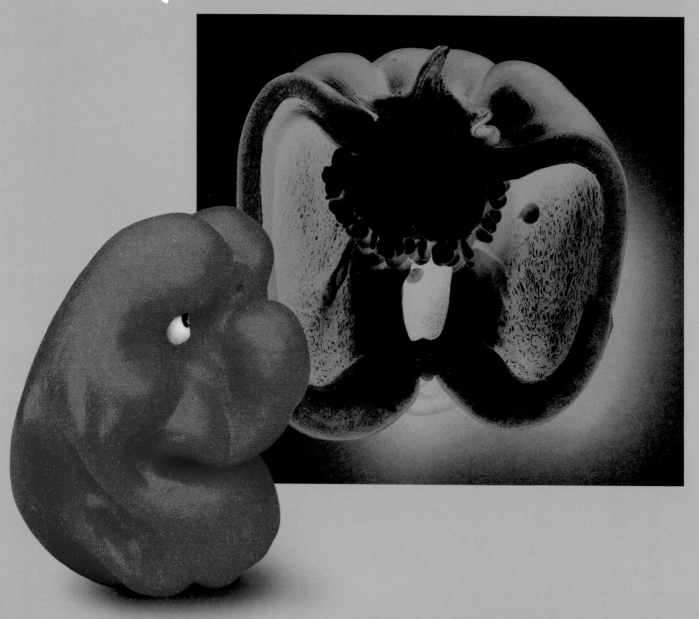

Y y

Yo-yo

Z z

Zebra

51

OPPOSITES

Up

Down

Big

Little

53

Happy

Sad

Hot

Cold

Near

Come

Far

Go

Give

Receive

57

Whisper

Shout

Awake

Asleep